# Trees and Shrubs
## of Virginia

# Trees and Shrubs of Virginia

Oscar W. Gupton and Fred C. Swope
Department of Biology
Virginia Military Institute

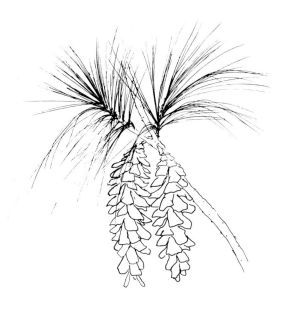

University Press of Virginia

Charlottesville

THE UNIVERSITY PRESS OF VIRGINIA
Copyright © 1981 by the Rector and Visitors
of the University of Virginia

*Second printing 1989*

Library of Congress Cataloging in Publication Data
Gupton, Oscar W
  Trees and shrubs of Virginia.
  Includes indexes.
    1. Trees—Virginia—Identification. 2. Shrubs—Virginia—Identification. I. Swope,
Fred C., joint author. II. Title.
QK484.V8G86     582.1609755     80–21585
ISBN 0–8139–0886–8

*Printed in Singapore*

To

Agnes and Clentis

# Contents

# Introduction

The trees and shrubs constitute one of the most important and distinctive elements of the surface of the earth. The ever-changing countenance of the land is a product of the variety, distribution, and life cycles of these woody plants. The various greens of summer are transformed into autumn's reds and golds, and then in the wake of the falling leaves appear the skeletons of winter.

Along with our enjoyment of the beauty and awesomeness of the seasonal changes there is the constant reminder of the measured pace of natural order. The ancient scheme is reflected by the plants in many ways. We see, for example, that every kind of living thing has its own timetable of events that leads up to preparations for the next generation; thus flowering and fruiting come not all at once but in a procession of varying colors, forms, and fragrances.

Just as there is a time for everything so is there a place. Plants do not grow just anywhere; particular species are associated with particular places, and we come to think of the willow with the stream, the spruce high on the mountain, and live oak near the sea.

Trees and shrubs stand as a canopy over most of the other forms of terrestrial life, and they characterize and control the natural communities of which they themselves are a part. Such is the influence of these dominant species that their loss sets in motion a chain of events that may completely alter the patterns of natural phenomena under their jurisdiction.

The realization that interference with this delicately balanced system, taken so much for granted, may have far-reaching and damaging consequences causes one to reflect upon the oftentimes injudicious use of natural resources and of the need to better understand these plants that are so great a part of the substance and majesty of our world.

Appreciation of and pleasure in these wild things are far more easily fostered when some knowledge of their characteristics is gained and their names are known. To this end some details of their structure, size, and color are herein supplied which, in combination with the photographs, furnish as direct a method as possible for identification.

The included species represent trees and shrubs from the mountains, piedmont, and coastal plain of Virginia. Some are indigenous to the area, and some are plants that have been introduced from elsewhere and have established themselves as members of our flora.

The descriptions that accompany each species are couched in nontechnical language requiring no knowledge of botanical terminology. The color photographs of each species were taken in the field under natural light conditions and are arranged by size, shape, and color of cone, flower, and fruit. Photograph size relative to actual plant size is noted.

One hundred species of plants that are classified as trees or shrubs have been described and photographed. These plants are representative of 77 genera and 40 families. There are 85 additional similar species cited with notes on their distinguishing features. An identification guide is therefore furnished for 185 species of woody plants, and since much of the surrounding territory is similar the guide is applicable far outside the state boundaries.

OSCAR W. GUPTON
FRED C. SWOPE

*Lexington, Virginia*

# Format

Each species is represented by two photographs, one showing the entire plant and one close-up of a cone, a flower, or a fruit. The plants are presented in three groups according to the subject of the close-up photograph.

First are the cone-bearing plants, arranged in order of cone size from largest to smallest.

The second group consists of those plants having a close-up photograph of the flower. Flowers of the same or similar color are placed together in five groups arranged in the following order: green or greenish; white; yellow; orange, pink, or red; blue, purple, or lavender. Within each color group the flowers are in order of the size from largest to smallest. In some instances densely clustered flowers that give the appearance of a single flower are treated as such.

The third group is made up of the species having a close-up photograph of the fruit. The arrangement is in order of fruit size from largest to smallest, and, though there is much variety, fruits of similar shape are placed together as closely as possible.

The information given for each species is in the same order throughout and is as follows:

Common name
*Scientific name* Flowering, fruiting, or cone-bearing period

Below each close-up photograph is a magnification symbol that indicates the size of the photograph relative to the actual size of the plant. The symbol × 2, for example, means that the size of the photograph is twice that of the plant; × 1 means that the photograph is the same size as the plant; and × ½ means that the photograph is one half the size of the plant.

Description:
   **Size and habit** are indicated by a statement of plant height and the species' status as tree or shrub.
   **Frequency** of the species is noted if it is found infrequently or rarely.

**Leaf character** is cited with respect to size, shape, arrangement, or other special quality.

**Flower or cone** features are described in terms of color variations, size, shape, or other character peculiar to the species.

**Fruit** size, shape, and color are given.

**Similar species** are cited, and distinguishing characters are given for purposes of identification.

**General comments** are included to note such things as particular uses made of plant materials, suitability for planting, etc.

**Habitat**, or the natural environment in which the plant is usually found, is noted as well as the geographic province. If no province is mentioned the species may be found in all three provinces: mountains, piedmont, and coastal plain. Provinces are marked on the map on page xiii.

Scientific names of the species follow the eighth edition of *Gray's Manual of Botany*. An index is included that places each species in the family to which it belongs and also provides a guide for pronunciation of the scientific names.

Botanical manuals that contain identification keys and additional technical information about these and other plants of the northeastern United States are listed below.

Fernald, M. L. 1950. *Gray's Manual of Botany*. Eighth edition. American Book Company.

Gleason, M. A. 1952. *Illustrated Flora of the Northeastern United States and Adjacent Canada*. The New York Botanical Garden.

Gleason, M. A., and A. Cronquist. 1963. *Manual of the Vascular Plants of Northeastern United States and Adjacent Canada*. D. Van Nostrand Company.

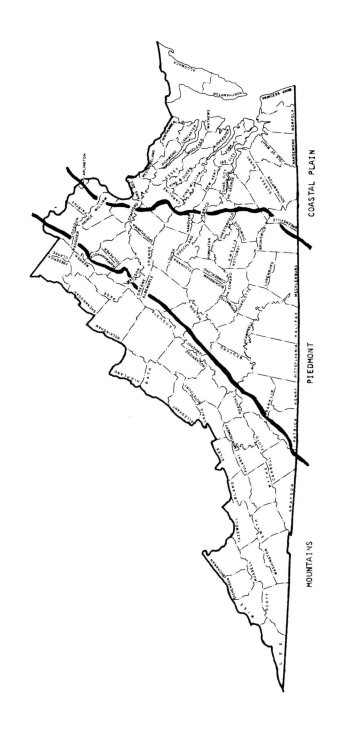

Trees and Shrubs
of Virginia

# White Pine

× ¾

*Pinus strobus*                                         August–September

This pine is an evergreen tree that grows to a height of over
200 feet. Much of the bark is smooth, unlike other pines,
and the branches develop in a whorled pattern. The pale
green needles are in groups of 5 and are about 3 to 5 inches
long. The elongate cones have no prickles and measure 4 to
6 inches in length. This is our only smooth-barked, smooth-
coned pine with needles in groups of 5. White Pine is a
valuable timber tree and important in reforestation. It is
often planted in yards and parks, but, more important, it is
a familiar contrasting element to the oak-hickory canopy of
the mountains. Lumbering and blister rust are problems.
*Dry or moist woods; chiefly mountains.*                      1

# Loblolly Pine

*Pinus taeda*                                    October–November

This evergreen tree is frequently 80 to 100 feet tall but can grow much taller. The needles are in groups of 3, pale to dark green, and are 5 to 10 inches long. The cones are 3 to 5 inches long with stout prickles. This species may resemble *P. serotina* or *P. rigida*, but it has larger cones than either of them. *P. australis* may occasionally be somewhat similar, but the needles are usually twice or more as long, and the cones are 6 to 10 inches in length. Loblolly is a fast-growing and important timber tree with strong, hard wood. It is an attractive tree that will grow well in compacted or loose soils with a wide range of moisture. *Low woods, old fields; piedmont, coastal plain.*

3

# Table Mountain Pine

*Pinus pungens*                                    September–November

This usually small evergreen tree with spreading branches
infrequently reaches a height of 60 feet or more. The needles
are usually in groups of 2 or occasionally 3 and are 1½ to 3
inches long. The needles are stiff and blue-green. Male cones
are about ½ inch long and in elongate clusters. The female
cones are oval to almost round, 2 to 4 inches long, and armed
with stout, hooked spines. The winged seeds are about ¾
inch long. Table Mountain Pine is a tree of poor soils in the
uplands and so affords vegetative cover in some rather barren
sites. *Dry, rocky soils; mountains.*

5

# Pitch Pine

× ¾

*Pinus rigida*                                    September–October

The irregularly spreading branches of this evergreen tree may be 70 to 80 feet from the ground, but usually the plant is of lesser stature. The stiff needles are in groups of 3 and are about 2 to 5⅓ inches long. The cones are about 1½ to 2½ inches long and conical or oval with short, slender prickles. *P. serotina* and *P. echinata* are similar pines; the former has needles 6 to 8 inches long and almost round cones, and the latter has needles in groups of 2 and 3. Pitch Pine wood is used as flooring timber, and the tree was an early source of resin in the turpentine industry. The species gives vegetative cover to areas of poor soil. *Dry, rocky, sandy soil.*

# Virginia Pine

$\times \frac{1}{2}$

*Pinus virginiana*                    September–November

This evergreen is usually a tree of 30 feet or less with spreading, drooping branches. The needles are ¾ inch to 3 inches long, twisted, and in groups of 2. The clustered male cones are ⅓ to ¾ inch long. Female cones are 1 ½ to 3 inches long and bear short, slender spines. The winged seeds are about ¾ inch long. *P. echinata* is similar, but the less twisted needles are in groups of 2 or 3 and are 3 to 5 inches long. Virginia Pine does well on almost any kind of poor soil and can add much to otherwise sparse tracts with its bushy habit and a growth form that frequently resembles bonsai. *Dry, rocky, or sandy soil.*

9

# Red Spruce

× ¾

*Picea rubens*                                    August–September

This is an evergreen tree of slender branches, pyramidal form, and a height of about 80 feet. The leaves are ½ to ¾ inch long, 4-sided, and leave a short, stalklike projection on the stem when they fall. The cones are about 1 inch to 2½ inches long, reddish brown, and hang from the stems. *P. abies*, a European introduction, is frequently planted and has drooping branches and cones 4 to 6 inches long. The firs, *Abies fraseri* and *A. balsamea*, have flat leaves and erect cones on the stems. Spruce is at about 4000 feet elevation and fir at about 5000 feet. These trees are distinctive landmarks of the higher mountains, but their populations have decreased. *Wooded slopes, balds; mountains.*

# Bald Cypress × ½

*Taxodium distichum* September–October

This tree may stand 150 feet, and the trunk is often enlarged at base. The narrow, pointed leaves are ½ to ¾ inch long in two rows on the stem. The globose cones hang from stem ends and are about 1 inch in diameter. *T. ascendens*, usually a more southern species, is a rarer tree with shorter, needlelike leaves pressed against the stem and peeling bark. Cypress, when growing in very wet soil or standing water, sends up root projections called "knees" that rise above the soil or water. The valuable wood is much used in construction and is highly resistant to weathering. Bald Cypress is a most striking feature of coastal swamps, especially when draped with Spanish Moss as shown here. *Swamps, stream borders; chiefly coastal plain.*

# Eastern Hemlock

× 1¼

*Tsuga canadensis*  September–November

This tall evergreen is pyramidal or conical in form and frequently stands nearly 100 feet. The small, narrow leaves are oblong and about ½ inch or less in length. The underside of the leaf is whitened or silvery. The cones are ¾ inch or less in length. *T. caroliniana* is a similar species that has leaves a little larger and cones about twice as long. Both of these hemlocks are among the most beautiful trees in our forests. Eastern Hemlock is more common, and its graceful colonies are the dominant feature of many mountain coves. The hemlock with which Socrates was poisoned is the herbaceous species, *Conium maculatum. Cool, moist slopes; chiefly mountains.*

15

# Arbor Vitae

*Thuja occidentalis*                               September–October

Arbor Vitae is an evergreen tree that grows to about 60 feet.
The bark is brown to reddish brown and is usually ridged.
The young stems are flattened toward the ends. The leaves
are small, overlapping scales about ⅛ inch long. The leafy
branches give the appearance of having been pressed. The
cones are ovoid, about ½ inch long, and have smooth, flat
scales. The seeds are winged. An oriental species, *T. orien-*
*talis*, is imported and planted frequently; it is distinguished
by its larger cones with a hooklike projection on the scales
and wingless seeds. Arbor Vitae wood is soft but durable for
use as posts. It is often planted in large gardens and has many
forms varying in shape and color. *Moist woods, stream banks*
*especially in limestone; mountains.*

17

# Red Cedar

× 1¼

*Juniperus virginiana*                    August–October

This is an evergreen shrub or tree highly variable in form
with a maximum height of about 90 feet. Stems are 4-sided
usually having tiny, overlapping, scalelike leaves, but frequently there are longer, slender-pointed leaves that do not
overlap. Leaves are fragrant and bluish to yellowish green or
reddish brown. Male cones are tiny and numerous at stem
ends. Female cones, on separate trees, are ¼ inch, blue, and
berrylike with a whitish, or "frosted," coating. *J. communis* is
a much rarer, low shrub with all leaves longer and not overlapping. Red Cedar is the alternate host for apple rust, which
leaves a round, reddish brown gall. Fence posts made from
this tree are very durable, and the aromatic wood is that of
cedar chests. *Dry soils, especially limestone.*

19

# Tulip Tree

*Liriodendron tulipifera*                                 May–June

A height of 150 to 190 feet may be attained by this tree. Leaves are 5 to 8 inches long and about as wide with a shallow notch at the tip. Flowers are green to yellow with orange marking within. The fruit is a brown, conelike structure about 3 inches long. It is valued as an ornamental and a shade tree. The trunk may develop a diameter of 10 feet, and the autumn color of the unusually shaped leaves is a brilliant yellow. The plant is extremely attractive where a large tree can be accommodated. There is little trouble with insect or fungal pests. This is an important timber tree as the wood is used in furniture and is easily worked. *Rich woods*.

# Cucumber Tree

*Magnolia acuminata*                                     May–June

This tree grows to a maximum height of about 90 feet. The large, pointed leaves may be 4 to 12 inches long and are often wider toward the tip. The flower color varies from yellow to yellowish green. The fruits are oblong, conelike structures bearing red seeds; the name of the plant comes from the cucumberlike shape. *M. fraseri* and *M. tripetala* differ from Cucumber Tree in that the former has lobed leaf bases; the latter has much larger, white flowers. The magnolias are hardy plants that are relatively pest-free, and the leaves, flowers, and fruits are very attractive. *Rich, wooded slopes; chiefly mountains, piedmont.*

# Strawberry Bush

× 1¼

*Euonymus americanus*                              May–June

This is a wide-branching shrub that grows from 3 to 6 feet tall. The toothed leaves are in pairs and are pointed at both ends. The small flowers are about ½ inch in diameter with 5 green or purplish petals. The fruit is bright red and covered with wartlike projections. *E. atropurpureus* is a similar plant with purplish brown flowers having only 4 petals and smooth, pinkish purple fruits. Although the foliage is attractive and persistent, it is often sparse, but in the autumn the bright fruits make for a plant of unusual beauty. *Moist to dry woods, thickets.*

# Wild Gooseberry

× 1½

*Ribes rotundifolium*                                    April–May

This shrub is 2 to 3 feet tall. Very short, slender spines may or may not be present on the stems. The lobed leaves are somewhat round in outline and from ½ inch to 2 inches in diameter. The small flowers are about ½ inch long and green or reddish green. The fruits are spherical, about ¼ to ½ inch in diameter, and purple. *R. cynosbati* and *R. glandulosum* are similar species but have prickly fruits, and the latter has an unpleasant odor when bruised. The cultivated gooseberry, or currant, is *R. sativum. Rich woods, open slopes; mountains.*

27

# Tree of Heaven

× ¼

*Ailanthus altissima*                                    July–October

This tall tree sometimes attains a height of 100 feet. The bark is moderately smooth and gray. The large leaves are 1 foot to 2½ feet long and divided into many oblong, pointed segments with a few teeth at their bases. The green or greenish yellow flowers are small but grow in large clusters 5 to 15 inches long. The winged fruits are 1 inch to 2 inches long with the seed in the middle. The color of the fruit varies from reddish brown or pink to copper-colored to bronze. This species is an Asian introduction that has become a part of our flora. It is a rapidly growing plant with all-around superior ornamental qualities, although there is some objection to the ill-scented flowers and aggressive growth. *Roadsides, clearings, open woods.*

29

# Smooth Sumac

*Rhus glabra*                                       June–October

This is a shrub from 2 to 30 feet tall with smooth stems. The large leaves are divided into 10 to 30 oval-pointed, toothed segments. The small, greenish yellow flowers grow in dense clusters at the ends of the stems. The small fruits are hairy, red globes in large, compact clusters. *R. typhina* and *R. co-pallina* are similar, but the former has hairy twigs and leaf stalks, while the latter has the stalk between leaf segments winged. *R. vernix*, which is very poisonous, has toothless leaf segments, loose flower clusters, and white fruits. The sumacs often grow in handsome colonies that are brilliant red in autumn, and the colorful fruits persist into winter. *Roadsides, fields, wood borders.*

31

# American Chestnut

× ¼

*Castanea dentata*

June–July

This tree, once a 100-foot member of our forests, now exists only in sapling form. The 5- to 12-inch leaves have bristle-tipped teeth and wedge-shaped bases. The dense tails of yellowish green flowers ornament the upper limbs. The fruits are nuts enclosed in a prickly burr. A fungal disease has all but eliminated this species, leaving only short-lived sprouts. The exotic species *C. mollissima* and *C. sativa* are frequently planted. They have hairy leaf stalks and undersides and leaf bases frequently rounded or squared off. American Chestnut was a valuable timber tree, and the edible nuts were market-able and highly valued. *Rich woods; chiefly mountains.*

33

# Mockernut

×½

*Carya tomentosa*                                                                                      April–May

This hickory may grow to a height of about 100 feet and has dark to light gray bark that is ridged or furrowed but does not peel off in sheets. The small stems are hairy. The leaves are 8 to 12 inches long and are divided into several oval and pointed segments with toothed margins. The tiny male flowers are in slender clusters 4 to 6 inches long. Female flowers are small and in inconspicuous groups at the ends of stems. The fruits are nuts enclosed in a thick husk 1 inch to 2 inches in diameter. Many hickories are somewhat similar. *C. ovalis* resembles Mockernut but the bark usually begins to peel off, leaves and stems are less hairy, and the fruit husk is thinner. The hickories are attractive trees and the tough wood is much used in the lumber trade. *Dry woods*.                                  35

## Cherry Birch

× ½

*Betula lenta*                                            April–May

This birch may attain a height of 70 to 80 feet. The aromatic bark is reddish brown, resembling cherry. The oval and pointed leaves have teeth and are 1 inch to 4 inches long. The very small male flowers are clustered in slender "tails" 2 to 4 inches long; females are shorter and thicker. Fruits are very small, flat disks. *B. lutea* is very similar but can be distinguished by its yellow bark; also it is usually found at higher elevations. *B. nigra* is somewhat similar but with more triangular leaves and hairy leaf stalks; it is mostly at lower elevations. The wood is strong and has been used in furniture manufacturing. A flavorful beverage is made from the fermented sap. *Rich woods; mountains, piedmont.*

37

# Silky Willow

*Salix sericea*                                    March–April

This shrub or small tree may be 3 to 15 feet tall. The narrow, pointed leaves are 1 inch to 5½ inches long with finely toothed margins and white hairs on the underside. The very small flowers are in dense clusters ½ inch to 1½ inches long that appear before the leaves. The fruits are tiny capsules less than ¼ inch long and ovoid. They also grow in dense clusters. *S. nigra* and *S. caroliniana* are also common willows, but both develop flowers along with the leaves. The former is without the white hairs beneath the leaves, which are frequently curved, while the latter's leaves have a whitish coating underneath that rubs off. *Wet lowgrounds and streamsides.*

# Weeping Willow

× 1

*Salix babylonica*                                                April–May

This tree with the "weeping" branches reaches a height of 40 feet. The narrow, pointed leaves are 1 inch to 5 inches in length. The very small flowers develop with the leaves in dense clusters ½ inch to 1½ inches long. The fruits are very small, ovoid capsules that also grow in dense clusters. *S. alba* and *S. fragilis* are somewhat similar but without conspicuously drooping branches, and the latter has wider leaves and brittle branches. All three of these willows are introductions that have escaped cultivation into our flora. The willows have great beauty and are easily planted by pushing a broken stem into moist soil. *Streamsides, moist roadsides.*

# Cane

*Arundinaria gigantea*                                    April–May

This is a shrub 2 to 30 feet tall that forms dense colonies.
The elongate, pointed leaves are 2 to 12 inches long. The
tiny flowers are enclosed in a series of flat, somewhat overlapping, pointed structures that are green, brown, or purplish.
The fruits are small grains about ½ inch or less in length.
Cane is most similar to the imported species of bamboo and
is a member of that group of grasses. Sometimes a second
species, *A. tecta*, is described as being smaller in stature, with
the flowers developing on leafless shoots. *Swamps and wet
woods.*

# Flowering Dogwood

*Cornus florida* March–June

This small tree may reach a height of almost 50 feet but is usually much smaller and often appears shrublike with multiple trunks. The spreading branches form a wide, rounded crown. The leaves are oval and pointed with the veins curving toward the tip, and they grow in pairs. The small flowers are white, greenish, or yellow and in small clusters surrounded by 4 rounded, modified leaves that are white, or ocassionally pink, and very showy. The red, oval fruits are in small clusters. *C. amomum* and *C. alternifolia* are smaller plants and shrubby without the showy modified leaves around the flower clusters, and the leaves of the latter are not in pairs. The Flowering Dogwood is perhaps the best known tree. *Woods*.

# Cigar Tree

*Catalpa speciosa*                                        May–June

This tree reaches about 100 feet in height. The large, heart-shaped leaves are 6 to 12 inches long and grow in pairs or frequently in whorls of 3. The flowers are white or off-white with yellow stripes and purple or purple-brown spots. The fruits are long, cylindrical structures 8 to 12 inches or more in length. *C. bignonioides* is native further south but is sometimes planted in the north, and the flowers are smaller with more conspicuous purple spotting. These trees are frequently planted as ornamentals for their large, handsome leaves and flowers and the curious "cigar" fruits. *Moist woods.*

# Sweet Bay

× ¾

*Magnolia virginiana*                                          May–July

This tall, near evergreen shrub or slender tree may grow to a
height of 30 feet. The thick, leathery leaves are white underneath, 3 to 6 inches long, narrowed at both ends, and frequently wider near the tip. The fragrant flowers are white to
cream with curved parts giving a globular form and measuring about 2 inches across. The conelike fruits are 1 inch to 2
inches long and reddish. This species has several desirable
features as an ornamental of moist situations. The large
leaves, glossy above and white beneath, and the white or
cream-colored floral spheres with their pleasant odor are excellent qualities. *Low woods, swamps; chiefly piedmont and
coastal plain.*

# White Rhododendron

×¾

*Rhododendron maximum*                                    June–July

The crooked stems of this shrub or small tree may be 25 to 30 feet tall. The large, evergreen leaves are 4 to 12 inches long and tapered at both ends. The white to deep pink flowers measure 2 to 2½ inches across. The oblong fruits are hairy capsules ½ to ¾ inch long. Leaves and flower color may occasionally resemble those of *R. catawbiense*, but that species usually has shorter leaves with rounded bases and much purple in the flower color. Both species are excellent choices for planting and are extensively so used. White Rhododendron is also known as Great Laurel. *Moist woods, stream and pond margins; mountains.*

51

# Buttonbush

× ½

*Cephalanthus occidentalis*          June–August

This spreading shrub ranges from about 3 to 12 feet in height. The oblong leaves are tapered to a point, measure about 2 to 8 inches in length, and grow in pairs or in threes along the stem. The small, white or cream flowers are densely clustered in a spherical formation about an inch in diameter. The small fruits are wedge-shaped and tightly clustered in spheres a little smaller than the flowering heads. It is infrequently planted as an ornamental in wet sites. *Stream and pond borders, marshes.*

# Fringe Tree

× ½

*Chionanthus virginicus*                                    May–June

This species is called both a large shrub and a small tree. The leaves are tapered at both ends, often wider near the tip, and are 3 to 8 inches long. Leaves are in pairs along the stem, and the veins are very conspicuous underneath. The fragrant flowers grow in numerous dense and drooping clusters. The fruits, about ½ inch long, are ovoid and dark blue. The rather large leaves and the graceful pendulous floral arrangement combine for a striking contribution to the spring landscape. It is frequently planted. *Moist or dry woods and bluffs.*

55

# Swamp Honeysuckle

×1

*Rhododendron viscosum*                                              June–July

This shrub of many branches is usually 3 to 10 feet tall. The leaves are about 1 inch to 2½ inches long, oval-shaped with a short, pointed tip and have the margins lined with fine hairs. The sticky flowers are usually white but occasionally have a pink tint and are fragrant. The fruits are elongate, hairy capsules about ½ inch long. *R. atlanticum*, a species of somewhat drier habitat, is similar but is of smaller stature, blooms earlier, and has white, pink, or purple flowers. The Swamp Honeysuckle is a fine plant of wet situations with attractive foliage, fragrance, and color for summer. *Swamps, bogs, pond and stream margins.*

57

# Black Locust

× ¾

*Robinia pseudo-acacia*                                       April–June

This tree may grow to a height of 80 feet and has thick, furrowed bark. The branches are thorny with the thorns usually occurring in pairs. The leaves are 7 to 12 inches long and divided into many small segments. The flowers hang in drooping clusters 4 to 8 inches long and are very fragrant. The fruits are elongated and flattened pods 2 to 4 inches long. The Honey Locust, *Gleditsia triacanthos*, is not similar, with its very small flowers, larger and frequently branched thorns, and fruits, which are also flattened pods but twice the size of Black Locust fruits. Black Locust is valued both as an ornamental and as a source of strong, hard wood, especially fence posts. *Woods and thickets*.

# Linden

× ½

*Tilia heterophylla*                                    June–July

This is a large tree growing to a height of about 100 feet. The large, oval-pointed leaves are toothed and are usually asymmetrically heart-shaped. The flowers and fruits are in clusters on a stalk that projects from a narrow leaf. Flower color varies from yellowish white to cream. The small fruits are oval to globular. *T. americana* is a very similar tree having the underside of the leaves darker green. The described species are so similar as to suggest one highly variable species. They are frequently planted in locations where their size can be accommodated. *Rich woods*.

# Morrow's Honeysuckle

× 1¼

*Lonicera morrowi*                                    May–June

This thickly branched shrub is 3 to 10 feet tall. The oval-pointed leaves are 1 inch to 2½ inches long and hairy underneath. The flowers are white, but many turn yellow. The fruits develop as red berries, and the plant is usually heavily fruited. *L. tatarica* is a similar species, but some flowers are pink or pinkish, and the leaves are not hairy underneath. Both of these plants are Eurasian introductions that have escaped cultivation and become established here. They are planted as ornamentals, often as hedges, for their colorful and abundant flowers and fruits. *Roadsides and wood borders.*

# Black Cherry

*Prunus serotina*

×½

April–June

This cherry may reach a height of 100 feet. Young branches are reddish brown and smooth. The oval or oblong pointed leaves have blunt, incurved teeth and a shiny upper surface. The elongate clusters of white flowers are dense and numerous. The small, dark purple or black cherries are edible when fully ripe. *P. virginiana* is a similar plant but is smaller and usually more shrubby; also the teeth of the leaves are sharper and do not curve inward. The fruits of Black Cherry have been used in making various beverages and jelly. The wood makes attractive furniture and paneling. *Dry woods, fence-rows.*

65

# Red Chokeberry

× 1¼

*Pyrus arbutifolia*                                        April–May

This shrub is 2 to 8 feet tall often forming large colonies. Young stems are usually very hairy. The leaves are 1 inch to 4 inches long with many small teeth and a pad of soft hairs underneath. Flower color may vary from white to pink. Flower clusters are 1 inch to 4 inches in diameter. The bright red fruits develop in berrylike clusters of 2 to 20. *P. melanocarpa* is similar, but the underside of the leaf has few or no hairs, and the fruit is black. The growth form may be somewhat straggling, but these shrubs, especially in colonies, are quite attractive in leaf, flower, and fruit. Foliage is red in autumn, and fruits persist through the winter. *Swamps, wet woods.*

67

# Autumn Olive

*Elaeagnus umbellata*
× 1
May–June

This spreading shrub, frequently with spiny branches, may be 10 to 12 feet tall. Smaller branches are often silvery. The oval, pointed leaves are silvery underneath and often have wavy margins. The yellowish white to white flowers are fragrant and grow in small clusters close to the stem. The oval fruits are silvery at first, later turning pink to red. *E. augustifolia* is a similar species but may grow to 25 feet in height; also the leaves are silvery on both sides, and the fruits are yellow. Both these plants are Asian introductions that have escaped from cultivation as ornamentals. *Roadsides, low woods, pastures.*

69

# Bladdernut

×1

*Staphylea trifolia*                              April–May

This is a shrub or small tree with striped bark. The leaves are in pairs along the stem and are divided into three equal segments that are pointed and toothed. The white to greenish white flowers are in short, drooping clusters. The fruits are three-parted, papery pods (the "bladders") that are air-filled except for the very few small seeds. The flowers, although not really showy, are attractive, and, along with the foliage and interesting form of the fruit, the plant adds to the variety of spring and fall beauty. *Moist woods and thickets.*                              71

# Sourwood

*Oxydendrum arboreum*                                        June–July

Sourwood grows to a height of about 65 to 75 feet. The leaves are 4 to 8 inches long tapering gradually to a point with the margins either smooth or with tiny teeth. A taste of the leaf reveals the source of the common name of the plant. The flowers are small and tubular or urn-shaped, growing in slender, one-sided clusters. Numerous clusters develop at the ends of the branches often when the tree is quite small. The fruits are about the shape and size of the flowers. The foliage and flowers are summer attractions, the flower shape and arrangement giving the name Lily of the Valley Tree. In autumn the leaves are bright red. *Wet or dry woods*.

73

# Deerberry

× 1

*Vaccinium stamineum*                                                May–June

This shrub is 1 foot to 6 feet tall. Leaves are 1½ to 4 inches long, oval or oblong, and pointed or blunt with a pale surface underneath. The flowers are usually numerous, and the wide spread of the petals makes the exposed yellow stamens conspicuous. The fruit is a berry about ½ inch in diameter and green, yellow, or blue. Deerberry differs from the other species in the blueberry group in that their flowers are tubular or urn-shaped. Deerberries are reportedly edible when cooked. *Dry woods.*

# Wild Hydrangea

× ¾

*Hydrangea arborescens*                              June–July

This shrub is usually 3 to 6 feet tall and has an irregular growth pattern. The oval and pointed leaves are in pairs with toothed margins. The flowers are in dense clusters at the ends of the stems. Flowers are usually very small, but occasionally some marginal ones are much larger and whiter. The fruits are very small, brown, urn-shaped, and with two protruding, stemlike tips. A showy form of this species with all the flowers of each cluster enlarged has been cultivated. Individual plants are generally scraggly, but colonies, especially along banks and ledges, are attractive. *Rich woods, rocky slopes, streamsides.*

77

# New Jersey Tea                                       × 1

*Ceanothus americanus*                              June–July

This low, freely branching shrub grows to about 3 feet. The pointed, finely toothed leaves are 1 inch to 3½ inches long and are often half again as wide. Three prominent veins branch from the base of the leaf, or frequently from a little below the blade on the leaf stalk. The small flowers are in numerous dense and showy clusters. The small fruits are 3-lobed and rounded, leaving a distinctive structure when they fall that resembles a golf tee. Much of the plant dies back in winter, and flowers are produced from new stems each year. The leaves were supposed to have been used as a substitute for tea during the Revolution. *Open woods and roadsides.*

# Black Haw

*Viburnum prunifolium*                                    April–May

Large shrub or small tree status is accorded this species. It may attain a height of 15 feet and has many stems branching at right angles. The fine-toothed leaves are oval in shape with pointed tips and grow in pairs along the stem. The small flowers grow in dense clusters 2 to 4 inches across. The fruits develop as clusters of black or blue-black, somewhat flattened balls. Two other species may appear similar. *V. rufidulum* has rust-colored leaves underneath, and *V. cassinoides* has larger leaves. The compact habit, foliage, numerous floral clusters, and attractive fruits combine several highly desirable qualities in Black Haw. *Dry woods and thickets.*

# Arrowwood

× ¾

*Viburnum dentatum*                                        June–July

This is a shrub 3 to 12 feet high. The toothed leaves are in pairs and vary from oblong or ovate to almost round; usually they taper abruptly to a point. The small flowers grow in conspicuous, usually flat-topped clusters at the ends of the stems. The fruits are oval, blue-black, and about ½ inch long. *V. rafinesquianum* is a similar species, but the leaves average larger, and the leaf stalks are very short, especially the upper ones. Arrowwood is a good choice for ornamental planting with attractive flowers, fruits, and foliage. It grows well in moist and dry places. *Streamsides, thickets, moist or dry woods.*

83

# Scotch Broom

× 1

*Cytisus scoparius*                                        April–June

The branches of this shrub are slender and green and reach a
height of 3 to 7 feet. The very small leaves are usually divided into 3 segments with some of the upper ones having
only one segment. The bright yellow flowers grow along the
upper ends of the stems. The fruits are flattened pods about
1½ to 2 inches long with hairy borders. This species was
introduced from Europe and is frequently planted. It grows
well in open areas and is quite attractive with its densely
branching stems and showy flowers. *Fields and roadsides.*

85

# Shrubby St. John's Wort

×1

*Hypericum spathulatum*                    June–August

This thickly branched shrub is generally 2 to 6 feet tall. The oblong, narrow leaves are tapered at both ends and occur in pairs. The bright yellow flowers are almost an inch across and occur singly or in small clusters. The central flower parts give a tassellike effect. The fruits are about ½ inch long and oval, splitting at the pointed tip. *H. densiflorum* is a similar shrub with somewhat wider leaves and smaller flowers arranged in a more or less flat-topped, dense cluster. Both these shrubs are attractive and tolerant of a wide range of environments. *Dry or moist woods, rocky or sandy slopes.*

# Bush Honeysuckle

$\times 1\frac{1}{4}$

*Diervilla lonicera*                                           June–July

This is a shrub $1\frac{1}{2}$ to 4 feet tall that frequently forms fairly extensive colonies. The oval, long-pointed leaves are in pairs and have fine teeth. The flowers are at first yellow but become suffused with red or purple. The fruit is a small capsule about $\frac{1}{2}$ inch long with a slender beak. *D. sessilifolia* is a very similar species that is much rarer; it has leaves either without or with very short leaf stalks. These plants are not plentiful but are seen as attractive patches of green and gold on some wooded slopes. *Dry or rocky woods and clearings; mountains.*

89

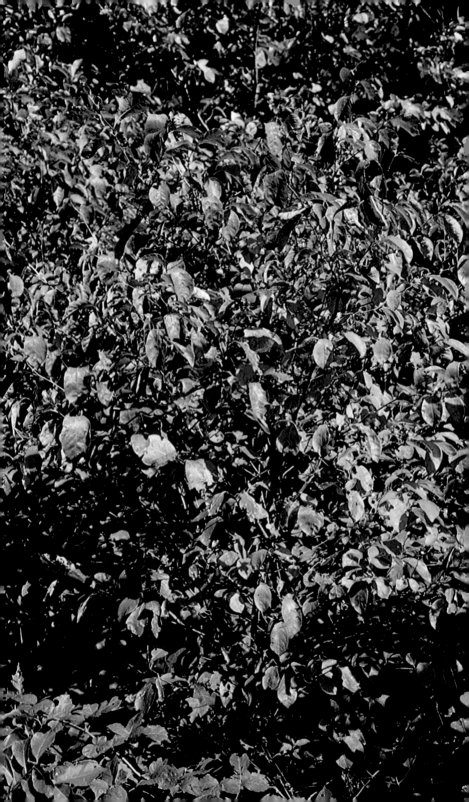

# Spicebush

×¾

*Lindera benzoin*                                         April–May

Spicebush is a shrub from 3 to 15 feet tall. The bruised stems and leaves are aromatic. The clusters of small yellow flowers close to the stem develop before the leaves appear. The oval fruits are bright red. The spicy fragrance is similar to that of Sassafras, a member of the same family; extracts of both plants have been used in beverage preparations. Spicebush is attractive in its early yellow floral display and late reds of autumn foliage and fruit. *Rich, moist woods and streamsides.*

# Sassafras

*Sassafras albidum*                                    April–May

This variable tree is usually of small to medium size, but it may appear shrublike or attain a height of over 100 feet. Broken stems are highly aromatic. The leaves may be all oval-shaped or a mixture of oval and lobed, either 3-lobed or in a mittenlike form. The yellow or greenish yellow flowers are small and develop in clusters at about the same time the leaves expand. The fruits are blue or blue-black, round to oblong, and about ½ inch long at the end of a red stalk. Root extract is used to make sassafras tea and other beverages. The flowers, fruits, and interestingly multiformed leaves that turn yellow, orange, and red in autumn make this a desirable tree for planting. *Woods, fields, roadsides.*

93

# Fragrant Sumac

*Rhus aromatica*                                          March–May

This small shrub grows from 1 foot to 6 feet tall, sometimes forming thickets. Leaves are in three parts with several rounded teeth on each side. Flowers are pale yellow and in short, spikelike clusters. Fruits are small, red, and berrylike, covered with tiny hairs and growing in tight clusters. The 3-parted leaves are somewhat similar to Poison Ivy or Poison Oak, but the fruit of these poisonous plants is white, and there is an additional difference in that Fragrant Sumac has an aromatic odor. The aroma, fruit color, and the red and orange autumn leaf color make for an ornamental shrub. *Dry, rocky woods; mountains, piedmont.*

95

## Pasture Rose

*Rosa carolina*                                          May–June

This low shrub is usually about 1 foot to 3 feet tall and sparsely branched. The stems bear straight, slender prickles. The leaves are divided into 3 to 7 oval and toothed segments. The usually solitary flowers vary slightly in color from pale pink to dark pink. The round, red fruits measure less than ½ inch in diameter. This species is very similar to *R. palustris*, which has curved prickles and flowers in small clusters. These species are summer attractions with their bright pink flowers and contribute to the fall color with the red fruits. *Roadsides, pastures, wood borders.*

# Flame Azalea

×¾

*Rhododendron calendulaceum* May–June

This freely branching shrub stands 3 to 12 feet tall. Leaves are oval and sometimes wider near tip; they tend to be crowded toward the stem ends. Leaves grow to a length of 2 to 4 inches but are immature at flowering. Flowers are in clusters of 3 to 12 and vary in color from yellow to orange to red. There is only one other species, *R. cumberlandense*, that approaches the color of this plant, and it blooms later, after the leaves are fully developed. The flower size, number, and color have made the Flame Azalea perhaps the most striking of our native shrubs. It is very frequently planted in yards, on campuses, and in parks. *Open mountain woods.*

# Early Azalea

*Rhododendron roseum*

× 1

May

Here is a shrub that grows to a height of about 10 feet. The leaves are 1 to 3 inches long, finely hairy, and often wider near the tip. The flowers are fragrant and usually deep pink but vary to pale pink or almost white. Fruits are hairy, narrowly oblong, pointed capsules that split open and remain on the plant into the winter. Two other similar species are *R. nudiflorum*, which flowers even earlier and has little or no fragrance, and *R. canescens*, which grows in moister areas of the coastal plain. Early Azalea is a handsome shrub with a combination of attractive foliage and bright, aromatic flowers. *Mountain woods.*

## Mountain Laurel

× 2¼

*Kalmia latifolia*                                      May–July

This large shrub or small tree is usually 3 to 10 feet tall but may grow much taller. The evergreen leaves are 2 to 5 inches long and pointed at both ends. The flower color may be pale pink, deep pink, reddish pink, pinkish purple, and occasionally white. The flowers are in large, showy clusters at the ends of stems. Fruits are small, somewhat flattened spheres that remain on the plant through the winter. *K. angustifolia* is somewhat similar but easily distinguished by the much smaller flowers; also the leaves are smaller and are in whorls of 3 along the stem. The Mountain Laurel is one of the most beautiful and hardy shrubs. *Rocky or sandy woods.*

# Bristly Locust

$\times \frac{1}{2}$

*Robinia hispida*                                                          May–June

This shrub is from 3 to 10 feet tall with coarse, bristly hairs on the stems. The leaves are 4 to 12 inches long and are divided into 6 to 15 round to oblong segments. There are elongate clusters of pink to purple flowers. The flattened fruits are pointed and bristly. A larger plant, *R. viscosa*, is without stem bristles and has pink flowers with a yellow spot. Colonies of Bristly Locust present a bank of bright pinkish purple when flowering and are sometimes planted as hedges. *Dry woods; mountains, piedmont.*

# Mimosa

×¾

*Albizzia julibrissin*                                    June–August

This spreading tree grows to a height of about 40 feet. The large leaves are 4 to 20 inches long and are divided into several featherlike parts that are in turn divided into many small, oblong pairs of segments. The clusters of small flowers with their numerous stamens resemble pink pin cushions, and the pink varies from very pale to very deep. The fruit is a flattened pod 3 to 7 inches long. Mimosa was introduced from Asia and has become established in many localities. It is widely planted for the singular effect of the pink floral mist and fernlike leaves. *Wood borders, clearings, roadsides.*

107

# Japanese Spiraea

× ¾

*Spiraea japonica*                                          June–July

The stems of this shrub may reach a height of 6 feet. The leaves are 3 to 6 inches long with toothed margins and taper to a slender point. The small, pink or red-pink flowers are in large clusters 2 to 8 inches across consisting of several aggregated smaller clusters. The fruits develop as clusters of tiny, inconspicuous, ovoid-pointed structures. *S. corymbosa* is somewhat similar but has generally paler pink or white flowers and shorter leaves. Both of these plants are attractive, medium-sized shrubs with good foliage and floral color and form. Japanese Spiraea was introduced and has escaped cultivation and established itself here. *Roadside banks, wood borders*.

# Purple Rhododendron

× ½

*Rhododendron catawbiense*                    May–June

This shrub or small tree may reach a height of 10 feet. The oval, evergreen leaves are rounded at both ends and are 3 to 6 inches long. The showy flowers occur in many clusters and vary in color from pinkish purple to purple. The fruits are oblong capsules with dense, reddish brown hairs. *R. maximum* may sometimes be similar, but, though the flowers may be deep pink, they are not purple, and the leaf bases are rarely rounded. Both of these rhododendrons are frequently planted, and Purple Rhododendron is considered by many to be our showiest shrub. *Mountain woods.*

111

# Purple-flowering Raspberry

*Rubus odoratus*                                    June–August

This raspberry is 3 to 6 feet tall, and the stems are without prickles. The 3- to 5-lobed leaves are toothed, are 4 to 8 inches across, and, unlike other raspberries, are not divided into several parts. The pinkish purple flowers are about 2 inches in diameter and resemble wild roses. The edible fruits are about ½ inch in diameter and red. Purple-flowering Raspberry is distinct from the other members of its group, since other raspberries and blackberries have prickled stems and leaves divided into smaller parts. This species grows very well in shady locations, and it is a highly attractive plant. *Wood borders, coves, moist roadsides; chiefly mountains.*

# Princess Tree

*Paulownia tomentosa*                          April–May

This introduced tree grows to a height of about 50 feet. The large, heart-shaped leaves are 6 to 12 inches long and often about as wide; they occur in pairs. The flowers are also large, 2 to 3 inches long, and appear before the leaves. The fruits are 1 inch to 2 inches long, ovoid, and pointed. These fruits remain on the tree through the winter along with the large buds of the next season's growth, supplying easy identification features. Princess Tree was introduced into this country from central China and has established itself in our flora. The size of the flowers and their growth in large clusters make this one of the showiest of trees in spring, and the large leaves are notable additions to summer foliage. *Woods, clearings, roadsides.*

115

# Pawpaw

× 1

*Asimina triloba*                                        April–May

This is a small tree 4 to 40 feet tall. Young stems have reddish brown hairs. Leaves are 6 to 10 inches long, usually a little wider toward the tip. When bruised the leaves have an unpleasant odor. The flowers appear with the leaves and grow from hairy stalks. The edible fruit is irregularly oblong, about 2 to 6 inches long, and yellowish green to brown. There is one other shrubby species, *A. parviflora*, that has smaller leaves, flowers, and fruits but is otherwise very similar. The leaf appearance along with the unusual flowers and fruits make this an interesting plant for decorative landscaping. *Low woods.*

117

# Wisteria

× ¼

*Wisteria sinensis*                                            May–June

This plant may grow as a shrub or twining vine. The large leaves may be 20 inches long and are divided into 7 to 13 segments. Flowers are blue, blue-violet, or occasionally white and form large clusters. The elongate fruit is 4 to 6 inches long and is covered with soft hairs that give a velvety texture. *W. floribunda*, another Asian introduction, like this species, is similar, but leaves are in 13 to 19 segments. *W. frutescens* is a native species without the hairs on the fruits. The introduced wisterias are used extensively as decorative plants and have escaped cultivation in many places; they are said to hybridize. *Open woods, wood borders, roadsides, fields; chiefly coastal plain.*

119

# China Tree

× ½

*Melia azedarach*                                                      April–May

This tree may be 50 feet tall and sometimes has an umbrellalike form. The large leaves are 10 to 30 inches long and composed of many toothed and pointed segments. The flowers are pale purple or pinkish purple. The round, greenish yellow or tan fruits are ¾ inch in diameter and have an unpleasant odor. The fruits are reported to be good insect repellants. China Tree is a naturalized Asian introduction that is a member of a family of great economic importance, since some of its species are sources of mahogany. *Roadsides, wood borders, fields; chiefly piedmont and coastal plain.*

121

## Osage Orange

× ¼

*Maclura pomifera*                              September–October

This tree grows to a height of 60 feet or more and has spreading, thorny branches that are sometimes tangled. The sap is milky and the wood yellow. The oval leaves narrow to a point and are about 2 to 6 inches long. The small flowers appear in small, inconspicuous, globose clusters, the males on one plant and females on another. The large fruits are produced in a form resembling a large orange or small grapefruit with a rough surface. The fruit color is green or yellowish green. This species was introduced from Texas and Arkansas. Root extracts have been used in dyes, and the American Indians are reported to have used the wood for bows. The trees have been frequently planted as hedges. *Roadsides, pastures, fence-rows.*

# Black Walnut

× ½

*Juglans nigra*

October

This large tree with brown, deeply furrowed bark grows to more than 150 feet. The large leaves are 1 foot to 2 feet long and are divided into many oval, toothed segments tapered to a slender point. The very small flowers, appearing before leaves are fully developed, grow in slender, elongate clusters 2 to 4 inches long. The fruits are globose about 1½ to 2½ inches in diameter. *J. cinerea* is a similar species but with oblong and sticky fruits. Black Walnut is an attractive large tree in foliage and stature, and the wood is most valuable, much used in furniture and gunstocks. *Rich woods.*

125

# Persimmon

× ½

*Diospyros virginiana*                    September–October

Persimmon is a tree that may attain a height of 50 feet. The dark bark is cleft into blocks. The oval or oblong leaves are pointed, often abruptly tapered, and are about 3 to 6 inches long. The tubular or urn-shaped flowers are yellow or greenish yellow, about ½ inch in length, and usually 4-petaled. The edible fruits are 1 inch to 1½ inches in diameter and vary in color from an orange or yellowish orange to purple. The fruits, or persimmons, are very astringent until after frost, whereupon they become quite sweet and tasty. The wood has had limited use in the making of golf clubs and billiard cues. *Dry woods, fields.*

# Sweet Gum

× ½

*Liquidambar styraciflua*                                    October

This tall tree grows to a height of nearly 150 feet. Bark frequently develops in wings on the stems. The leaves are star-like with 5 pointed and toothed lobes. The very small, greenish flowers are in globular clusters. The fruits develop into spherical, spiny structures that remain on the tree into the winter. The leaves resemble some maple leaves, but the latter grow in pairs on the stem. Twigs are sometimes chewed for the pleasant taste and odor of the aromatic gum. The wood is used in furniture manufacture for the high polish obtainable, and there are few trees that have more to recommend them as ornamentals. The large, lustrous, star-shaped leaves, rich green in summer and several shades of red and gold in autumn, are difficult to match. *Low, moist woods; piedmont, coastal plain.*

# Sycamore

*Platanus occidentalis*                          September–October

This tall, large tree grows to almost 180 feet in height with a diameter of over 10 feet. The trunk and branches are green, gray, white, or a combination of these due to the peeling bark. The large leaves are usually 3- to 5-lobed with large teeth and are often nearly circular in outline. The very small, inconspicuous flowers are in globular clusters. The fruits develop as balls 1 inch to 1½ inches in diameter on long stalks. Sycamore is the most massive of our woody plants. It is a handsome tree with or without foliage and is often planted for shade and ornament. *Low moist woods.*

# Chinquapin

× ½

*Castanea pumila*                                            August–October

This plant is usually shrubby but may be a small tree about 25 feet high. The toothed leaves are oblong, tapered abruptly to a point or rounded tip, and are hairy underneath. The very small flowers are crowded in elongate clusters 2 to 6 inches long. Each fruit, a nut, is enclosed in a prickly burr. *C. dentata* is similar in general appearance, but the leaves are usually longer, more sharply pointed, and without hairs underneath. The Chinquapin nuts are sweet and are occasionally marketed. This species offers good possibilities as an ornamental shrub as it is attractive in leaf, flower, and fruit and grows well in dry sites. *Dry woods, thickets.*            133

# Beech

× ¾

*Fagus grandifolia*                    September–October

Beech is a large tree that reaches 120 to 130 feet and has extremely smooth, light gray bark. The leaves are 2 to 5½ inches long, oblong and tapered to a point, and are toothed. The small flowers are inconspicuous. The male flowers are in small clusters on drooping stalks; the females are in pairs on shorter, thicker stalks. The fruit is a triangular nut enclosed in a spiny cover that remains on the tree long after the nuts have fallen. A European species, *F. sylvatica*, is often planted and has darker foliage with fewer and smaller teeth. The wood is used for veneer and furniture, and the bark is used, unfortunately, by those who feel it necessary to carve their initials. *Rich, moist woods.*

135

# Common Alder

× ½

*Alnus serrulata*                                    February—March

This shrub may attain a height of 15 feet. The leaves are oval
with a blunt point or rounded tip, usually widest near the
middle but often nearer the tip. The leaf margins are finely
toothed. The male flowers are formed in long, slender and
drooping clusters and the females in short, ovoid and erect
clusters. The very small fruits are nuts borne in a woody,
conelike structure that remains on the plant through the
winter. This shrub grows in dense colonies forming natural
hedgerows and may be planted in wet areas for this purpose.
*Streamsides, marshes, wet woods.*

# Sweet Fern

×1¼

*Comptonia peregrina*                              April–May

This aromatic shrub may attain a height of 5 feet but is usually about 1 foot to 3 feet. The fernlike leaves are narrow and elongate with the margins notched. The leaves are especially fragrant when bruised or broken. The male flowers are tiny in cylindrical clusters, while the females are in globose, bristly clusters. The fruits are very small brown nuts surrounded by a burr. Fairly large colonies occur that form dense mats ideal for covering banks or open areas. The fernlike appearance of the scented leaves is quite attractive. *Dry, open areas, steep rocky slopes; chiefly mountains.*

139

# White Oak

×½

*Quercus alba*                                    September–November

This large oak grows to be about 150 feet tall with a trunk
diameter of almost 10 feet. The bark is light gray or sometimes almost white. The leaves have usually 6 to 8 shallow
to deep lobes, these sometimes with smaller lobes. Leaves are
essentially smooth or hairless and without bristles at the lobe
tips. The flowers develop when the leaves are not fully expanded. The male flowers are yellow and develop in slender
clusters 2 to 3 inches long. The fruit, or acorn, is ½ to 1
inch long, the base covered by a shallow cup. *Q. stellata* may
be somewhat similar, but the leaves have fewer, almost
squared lobes as well as acorns half-covered by their cups.
The tough, strong wood of White Oak is highly valued for
many building purposes. *Rich or dry woods*.                141

# Bear Oak

× ¾

*Quercus ilicifolia*                                                  August

This species of oak is almost always a shrub that occasionally reaches a height of 15 to 20 feet. The leaves usually have 5 lobes with bristles at the tips and are 2 to 6 inches long. The male flowers are tiny and are produced in slender, stringlike clusters 2 to 5 inches long. The fruits, or acorns, are ½ to ¾ inch long in a cup covering about half the acorn. This is our only oak that is usually confined to growth as a low shrub. It does extremely well on exposed, steep slopes, and frequently forms very dense colonies. *Dry, rocky banks; mountains.*

143

# Pin Oak

×½

*Quercus palustris*                    October–November

Pin Oak may reach a height of 100 feet or more with spreading branches. The lower branches are usually slanted groundward. The glossy leaves have 5 to 7 lobes that usually have 3 bristle-tipped teeth. The leaf underside is smooth except for tufts of hairs where veins branch. Flowers are tiny and borne in elongate clusters 1 inch to 2 inches long. The fruits, or acorns, are about ½ inch long with the cup covering a third or less. *Q. coccinea* is a similar oak that has larger acorns and much less conspicuous tufts of hair on the undersides of the leaves. The hard, tough wood of Pin Oak is used in construction and has been used for shingles. It is a commonly planted tree for shade and ornament. *Wet woods.*

145

# Live Oak

×¾

*Quercus virginiana*                    September–November

This evergreen oak may become a large tree approaching 100 feet in height, but it is usually a small to medium tree with very widely spreading branches. The thick, tough leaves are 1½ to 3 inches long, sometimes wider nearer the tip, and occasionally with a few teeth. The margins of the leaves are usually turned under. The small flowers appear in slender, elongate, yellowish clusters. The fruit, or acorn, is about ½ to 1 inch long with the cup covering about a third of the base. *Q. laurifolia* is similar, but the leaves are not turned under and are usually bristle-tipped; the plant is not fully evergreen. Live Oak is often planted as an ornamental and shade tree. Often the growth pattern is reminiscent of bonsai. *Sandy coastal soils.*

147

# Red Mulberry

× ½

*Morus rubra*                                    June–August

This tree is often small or medium in size but may stand about 70 feet tall. The toothed, pointed leaves are oval or heart-shaped, occasionally lobed, and hairy underneath. The small male and female flowers appear with the leaves in slender clusters ½ inch to 2 inches long. The red or dark purple fruits are ½ inch to 2½ inches long, resembling blackberries. *M. alba* has white, pink, or purple fruits that are usually shorter and smoother; leaves are much more frequently lobed. *Broussonetia papyrifera* has rougher leaves than either of the above species, and the stems are very hairy. Fruits of the first two plants are sweet and edible. *Rich woods*.

# Witch Hazel

×¾

*Hamamelis virginiana*　　　　　　　　October–November

This shrub or small tree often reaches a height of 15 feet and is usually of widely spreading habit. The oval to almost round leaves may be blunt or pointed at the tip, the margins scalloped, and the base oblique or unequal. The yellow, or occasionally reddish, flowers appear in the fall and grow in very small clusters along the stem. Petals are narrow and ribbonlike. The fruits are odd-shaped woody structures somewhat wedge-shaped from which the seeds "explode" when ripe. The lotion called witch hazel is prepared from the bark. Some say the sound of the seeds hitting dead leaves led to the name of the plant. There is an insect gall frequently found on the leaves which has a conical shape like the crown of a witch's hat. *Woods*.

# Serviceberry

*Amelanchier arborea* May–June

This large shrub or small tree may be 35 feet tall. The oblong, pointed leaves have fine-toothed margins and are not fully expanded at flowering time. The flowers have narrow, straplike petals and develop in elongate, often drooping clusters while the leaves are still folded. Fruits are pinkish red to purplish red. There are several Serviceberries, easily recognized as such, but separation of species is difficult. These are striking plants of spring with numerous flowers that are highly visible due to the immature leaf condition. Shadbush is another popular name. *Woods, clearings, thickets; mountains, piedmont.*

153

# Black Gum

× ¾

*Nyssa sylvatica*                    September–October

This tree may be 100 feet tall. The leaves are oval, often wider towards the tip, and frequently narrowed to an abrupt point. The male and female flowers are tiny and inconspicuous, occurring in stalked clusters. The fruits are dark blue or blue-black and oval, commonly in threes on a 2- to 3-inch stalk. A variety of this species, *N. sylvatica* var. *biflora*, of swamps and wet woods, has narrow, oblong leaves, fruits usually in pairs, and trunk bases often enlarged. *N. aquatica* has larger leaves and fruits about 1 inch to 1½ inches in length, or about double that of Black Gum. The wood of Black Gum is an important timber item much used in furniture manufacture, and in moist sites the ornamental possibilities are great. Leaves are bright red in the autumn. *Woods, swamps.*

# Cottonwood

×½

*Populus deltoides*                              May–June

This is a tall, wide-branching tree that grows to well over 100 feet. The toothed leaves are triangular, heart-shaped, or oval and about as wide as long. The leaf stalks are flattened. The very small flowers are in slender and elongate clusters. The oval, pointed fruits are about ½ inch long in clusters 6 to 10 inches long. The seeds are covered by long silver hairs. *P. grandidentata* has leaves with fewer and larger teeth. *P. heterophylla* and *P. alba* both have rounded leaf stalks; the latter has leaves white-hairy underneath and fewer, blunt teeth. Cottonwood has been frequently planted for its rapid growth and attractive foliage, and the pendulous fruit clusters have brought the name Necklace Poplar. *Low woods, streamsides, swamps.*

157

# American Holly

*Ilex opaca*                                   September–October

This evergreen tree may be nearly 50 feet tall with light gray
or almost white bark. The stiff, leathery leaves are oval with
1 to several teeth tipped with sharp spines. The small, white
flowers are in clusters at the base of leaf stalks or small
branches. Male and female flowers are usually on separate
trees. The bright red fruits are round and about ¼ to ½ inch
in diameter, remaining on the tree through the winter. The
combination of rich, evergreen leaves and colorful fruits persistent into winter results in heavy collecting, especially at
Christmas, that is far too much for a slow-growing tree.
*Moist, dry, or sandy woods; chiefly piedmont and coastal plain.*       159

# Pagoda Dogwood

× ½

*Cornus alternifolia*

August–September

This dogwood is usually a shrub but may be a 25-foot tree. The branches spread horizontally in whorls, giving a tiered effect. The leaves are oval, narrowed abruptly to a point, and the veins are curved toward the tip of the leaf. Leaves, as well as branches, are not in pairs, or opposite one another, as are the other dogwoods. The small flowers are in flat or rounded clusters at the ends of stems. The dark blue fruits are round growing upon red stalks. *C. amomum* is generally similar, but the leaves and branches are paired or opposite one another, and the fruits are usually a paler blue. *Rich woods, rocky slopes, low roadsides; mountains, coastal plain.*

161

# Coralberry

*Symphoricarpos orbiculatus*                    September–December

This shrub is usually 2 to 3 feet tall but may grow much taller. It frequently forms dense colonies. The paired leaves are oval to almost round, hairy on the underside, and about 1 inch to 1½ inches long. The small flowers are in clusters close to the stems and vary from green to pink or pink-purple. The purplish red fruits are round, about ¼ inch in diameter, borne in dense clusters toward the upper ends of the stems. Fruits persist through the winter. A much rarer species, *S. albus*, has white or pink flowers and larger, white fruit. Coralberry does well in dry, exposed, and disturbed areas; the thick colonies are attractive and can be used in erosion control. *Moist to dry woods, roadsides, fields.*          163

# Sugarberry

× ½

*Celtis laevigata*                    August–October

This medium to large tree may be 90 feet tall. The bark is light gray and smooth except for scattered warty projections. The smooth-margined or few-toothed leaves are usually tapered to a slender point, and the leaf bases are generally rounded, often obliquely, with 3 conspicuous veins. The very small, green or greenish white flowers are inconspicuous, appearing in small clusters or singly. The fruits are small, almost round, and orange, red, or red-purple. *C. occidentalis* is similar, but the leaves are usually more rounded, toothed, and oblique at the base, and the fruits have a beak, or small, stemlike projection at the end. The bark, bright green leaves, and spreading branches make Sugarberry an attractive species for planting in a spacious plot. *Low, moist woods; coastal plain.*

165

# Ninebark

×¾

*Physocarpus opulifolius*  May–July

This shrub attains a height of 10 feet and has bark that usually peels off in strips. The leaves are usually 3-lobed and irregularly toothed. The flowers are produced in numerous dense clusters; the color is white varying to pale pink. The fruits are small, brown to purplish brown, teardrop-shaped pods. Species of *Ribes* have leaves similar to Ninebark, but stems of the latter are never spiny, and the flowers and fruits are quite different. The leaves, general habit, and abundant and colorful flowers and fruits make this plant very satisfactory for planting. *Sandy or rocky stream banks, wet woods.*

167

# Mountain Ash

× ½

*Pyrus americana*                                                                     May–June

This large shrub or small tree grows to a height of about 30 feet. The large leaves are divided into many toothed, oblong segments tapered gradually or abruptly to a sharp or blunt point. The small flowers are in dense clusters measuring 4 to 8 inches across. The fruits develop in bright red or orange-red rounded or flat-topped clusters. *P. aucuparia* is an introduced species often planted that sometimes spreads from cultivation. It differs from Mountain Ash in having hairy leaves and a little larger and more rounded petals along with somewhat larger fruits. Mountain Ash is a particularly decorative plant in form, foliage, flower, and fruit. *Mountain woods and open areas.*

169

# Devil's Walking Stick

× ¼

*Aralia spinosa*                              August–September

This prickly plant may be shrubby or a small tree to 30 feet with numerous strong prickles on stems and leaves. The extremely large leaves range up to 3 feet in length, 1 foot to 2 feet in width, and are divided into many oval, pointed, and toothed segments. The numerous small flowers are in great clusters made up of many smaller clusters. The ovoid, black fruits develop in equally large and numerous clusters. This is a striking species in every respect. The form, color, and size of the huge leaves, flower and fruit clusters, and the overall size of the plant lend an exotic effect wherever planted. *Rich or wet woods, steep slopes, low roadsides; chiefly coastal plain.*

171

# Elderberry

× ½

*Sambucus canadensis*                    August–September

This shrub is usually 3 to 10 feet tall but may reach 20 feet. The large leaves are in pairs and divided into oval-pointed segments having small teeth. The small flowers grow in large, flat-topped clusters at stem ends. The fruits are round and purple or black. *S. pubens* has red fruits, and the flowering and fruiting clusters are oval or pyramidal in form. The fruits of Elderberry are used in making wine and jelly. The plant is an attractive choice for its foliage, flower, and fruit. *Moist open areas.*                    173

# Wax Myrtle

× ½

*Myrica cerifera*                    August–October

This evergreen shrub or small tree is usually 3 to 30 feet tall.
The aromatic leaves are narrowed to the base and are usually
wider near the tip. Leaf margins are sometimes toothed, and
both surfaces have resinous droplets. The flowers are tiny in
very small and inconspicuous clusters. Fruits are round,
about ⅛ inch in diameter, and coated with a white or pale
gray waxy substance. *M. heterophylla* and *M. pensylvanica* are
very similar species having leaves more rounded and widened
at the tip as well as larger fruits; the latter's fruits are ¼ inch
in diameter, and leaf margins are turned under. The waxy
fruit coating is used in making fragrant candles. *Sandy soil,
marshes; coastal plain.*                    175

# Redbud

× ¼

*Cercis canadensis*                                                  March–May

This plant is a small tree that ranges from 15 to 40 feet in height and branches widely. Leaves are heart-shaped and appear after the flowers. The flowers are pink to pink-purple and in numerous clusters of 2 to 8. The fruit is a flat pod pointed at both ends, resembling a thin lima bean fruit; it develops a reddish to purplish bronze color. There are two western redbuds, but the only similar plant seen in this area is usually the imported *C. chinensis*, an Asian species with more rounded leaves. The early, bright, and abundant flowers and the attractive foliage recommend it as an ornamental. The name Judas Tree is also used in reference to the belief that Judas Iscariot hanged himself on a similar tree, perhaps the Eurasian *C. siliquastrum*. *Woodlands*.

177

# Ash-leaved Maple

× ½

*Acer negundo*                                                    May–October

This is a medium to large tree that may reach a height of 70
feet. The young stems are smooth and bright green. Leaves
are divided into 3 to 5 oval, pointed segments that have irregular teeth. The small flowers are green or yellow in drooping clusters that develop with the first leaves. The fruits are
winged and fused in pairs with the wings at an acute angle.
This tree is also known as Box Elder and is our only maple
with the leaves divided into several parts. It is frequently
planted along roadsides and in parks. The wood is not strong
but has been used to some extent for furniture. *Moist woods,
streamsides.*

# Sugar Maple

×¾

*Acer saccharum* June–September

This tree grows to a height of 120 or 130 feet. The leaves are in pairs, 3 to 7 inches long and about as wide, with 3 to 5 lobes and several large teeth. The yellow to greenish yellow flowers develop with the leaves in drooping clusters at the ends of the stems. The winged fruits are fused in pairs; each fruit is about 1½ inches long and fused at about a 60- to 70-degree angle to the other. *A. platanoides* is a similar species distinguished by milky sap, fruits fused in a straight line, and, usually, yellow autumn color. Sugar Maple wood is valuable in housing construction and furniture, and the sap is the source of maple syrup. The yellow, orange, and red foliage is a major contributor to autumn color. *Rich, wooded slopes; chiefly mountains.*

# Red Maple

× 1

*Acer rubrum*  May–June

This maple is usually small or medium in size but may be
100 feet tall. The lobed and toothed leaves are 2½ to 6
inches long and about as wide with a whitened underside.
The small, red flowers develop in clusters before the leaves.
The winged fruits are fused in pairs and are dull to bright
red. The leaves of *A. saccharinum* may be similar but are more
deeply lobed, and the flowers, fruits, and autumn leaves are
not red. Red Maple is a beautiful tree from early spring until
autumn in both form and color as it presents first red, then
green, and again red. *Moist woods.*

183

# Striped Maple

*Acer pensylvanicum*                                      May–June

A height of 30 to 40 feet may be attained by this small tree. The 3-lobed, finely toothed leaves are in pairs along the stem. The strings of small flowers may vary in color from yellowish green to bright yellow. The fruits appear as a pair of fused, winglike structures. A similar species is *A. spicatum*, but its leaves have larger and far more irregular teeth; flowers are on an erect stalk. *Viburnum acerifolium* may sometimes resemble Striped Maple, but the leaves of the former are usually characterized by fewer and blunter teeth; flowers are white and fruits black and not winged. Striped Maple is an attractive plant that does well in shade. *Rich mountain woods.*

# Mountain Maple

*Acer spicatum*                                     July–October

This is a large shrub or small tree 10 to 30 feet tall. The dark green leaves are 3- to 5-lobed and toothed; they measure about 3 to 5 inches in length. The greenish yellow flowers are crowded on erect stalks 2 to 4 inches long. The fruits are winged structures about 1 inch long and fused in pairs. *A. pensylvanicum* is somewhat similar, but it differs in having finer leaf teeth and drooping flower clusters. Mountain Maple often forms a rich, dense colony of dark green foliage on high peaks. *Rich woods, rocky slopes; mountains.*

# White Ash

×¼

*Fraxinus americana*                    August–October

This large tree may reach a height of 120 to 130 feet. The large leaves are in pairs and are divided usually into 7 toothed, oval-pointed segments. The tiny, inconspicuous flowers are in elongate clusters. The fruits are narrow, oblong, winged structures 1 inch to 2 inches long that hang in dense clusters. The ashes are all similar trees. The fruit wing of *F. pensylvanica* extends more around the swollen base; in *F. caroliniana* the wing almost encloses the base. Fruits of *F. tomentosa* are larger than the others, and leaf segments of *F. nigra* have no stalks. Wood of the ashes is strong and tough and is used extensively. Overall beauty of form and pest-freeness recommend them for planting. *Rich woods.*

189

# American Hazelnut

× ½

*Corylus americana*  August–September

The densely clustered stems develop into a thickly branched shrub from 3 to 10 feet high. The oval-pointed leaves are toothed, 2 to 6 inches long and often almost as wide; the stalks are hairy. The very small male flowers are in slender, conelike structures. The fruits are round nuts enclosed by small, toothed leaves that flare at the tips. *C. cornuta* is a similar shrub with hairy leaf stalks and fruits enclosed by leaves formed into an elongate beak. Both of these species have sweet, edible nuts. These shrubs frequently form fairly extensive thickets. *Woods, wood borders, roadsides, clearings.*

191

# Hornbeam

*Carpinus caroliniana*

×¾

August–October

This small tree may be 30 feet tall. The bark is gray and smooth with rounded ridges. The toothed leaves are oblong, tapering to a point, and about 2 to 5 inches long. Male and female flowers are very small and grow in slender, elongate clusters ½ inch to 1½ inches long. The fruiting structure appears as a string of arrowheadlike small leaves about 1 inch to 2 inches long. *Ostrya virginiana* is very similar in general form and leaf appearance, but the bark is brown and scaly, and the fruiting structure consists of a series of sacklike enclosures around the small fruits, each with a tuft of stiff hairs at the base. Both of these species are excellent ornamentals with full, bushy growth and attractive leaves and fruits. *Rich woods, streamsides.*

193

# Wafer Ash

*Ptelea trifoliata*                    August–September

The habit of this infrequent plant is usually shrubby, but it may be a small tree about 10 feet tall. The long-stalked leaves are divided into three segments that are oval-pointed with a very few to many small teeth. The small, greenish white to yellowish white flowers are in clusters at the ends of the stems. The fruits develop in dense bunches of papery, disklike structures almost circular in outline and often with a notch at the end. The foliage and fruits are attractive, and the species is sometimes cultivated to contrast with the more common shrubbery plantings. *Moist woods, thickets, rocky slopes; chiefly mountains and coastal plain.*

195

# American Elm

× 1¾

*Ulmus americana*                                    March–April

This tree often grows to a height of 100 feet or more. The leaves are oval, toothed, abruptly pointed, and 3 to 6 inches long. The bases of the leaves are often asymmetrical. The small, inconspicuous flower clusters develop long before the leaves. The fruits are disklike with a hairy border and a notch at the end. *U. rubra* is a smaller, similar tree with leaves usually rougher on the upper side, flower clusters much more dense and compact, and fruits without the hairy border. *U. alata* is also a smaller tree with much smaller, smoother leaves, oblong fruits hairy all over, and smaller stems frequently winged. American Elm has been a major ornamental and shade tree, but Dutch Elm Disease is a serious problem. *Rich, moist woods.*

# Sea Myrtle

× ¾

*Baccharis halimifolia*                    October–November

This thickly branched shrub is 3 to 12 feet tall. The oval or diamond-shaped leaves are usually more or less pointed at both ends, and the tips are toothed and sometimes wider than the bases. The tiny white or yellowish white flowers are in small, dense heads that resemble a single flower; these heads are arranged in larger, looser clusters. The small fruits develop tufts of white hairs. The numerous clusters of densely crowded fruits with their showy hairs give these shrubs the appearance of having large white or silvery flowers. *Marshes, thickets, wood borders, fields; coastal plain.*

199

# Index of Families and Pronunciation Key

The symbols ` and ´ mark the syllable to be accented; the former calls for a long vowel sound, while the latter calls for a short vowel sound.

Aceràceae (Maple Family)
  *Acer negúndo*
  *Acer pensylvánicum*
  *Acer rùbrum*
  *Acer sáccharum*
  *Acer spicàtum*
Anacardiàceae (Cashew Family)
  *Rhùs aromática*
  *Rhus glàbra*
Annonàceae (Custard Apple Family)
  *Asímina triloba*
Aquifoliàceae (Holly Family)
  *Ìlex opàca*
Araliàceae (Ginseng Family)
  *Aràlia spinòsa*
Bignoniàceae (Bignonia Family)
  *Catálpa speciòsa*
Caprifoliàceae (Honeysuckle Family)
  *Diervílla lonícera*
  *Lonícera mórrowi*
  *Sambùcus canadénsis*
  *Symphoricárpos orbiculàtus*
  *Vibúrnum dentàtum*
  *Vibúrnum prunifòlium*
Celastràceae (Staff Tree Family)
  *Euónymus americànus*
Compósitae (Composite Family)
  *Báccharis halimifòlia*
Cornàceae (Dogwood Family)
  *Córnus alternifòlia*
  *Córnus flórida*
Corylàceae (Hazel Family)
  *Álnus serrulàta*
  *Bétula lénta*
  *Carpìnus caroliniàna*
  *Córylus americàna*

Ebenàceae (Ebony Family)
  *Diospỳros virginiàna*
Elaeagnàceae (Oleaster Family)
  *Elaeágnus umbellàta*
Ericàceae (Heath Family)
  *Kálmia latifòlia*
  *Oxydéndrum arbòreum*
  *Rhododéndron calendulàceum*
  *Rhododéndron catawbiénse*
  *Rhododéndron máximum*
  *Rhododéndron ròseum*
  *Rhododéndron viscòsum*
  *Vaccìnium stamíneum*
Fagàceae (Beech Family)
  *Castànea dentàta*
  *Castànea pùmila*
  *Fàgus grandifòlia*
  *Quércus álba*
  *Quércus ilicifòlia*
  *Quércus palústris*
  *Quércus virginiàna*
Gramíneae (Grass Family)
  *Arundinària gigantèa*
Guttíferae (St. John's Wort Family)
  *Hperìcum spathulàtum*
Hamamelidàceae (Witch Hazel Family)
  *Hamamèlis virginiàna*
  *Liquidámbar styracíflua*
Juglandàceae (Walnut Family)
  *Càrya tomentòsa*
  *Jùglans nìgra*
Lauràceae (Laurel Family)
  *Líndera benzòin*
  *Sássafras álbidum*
Leguminòsae (Pulse Family)
  *Albízzia julibríssin*
  *Cércis canadénsis*
  *Cýtisus scopàrius*
  *Robínia híspida*
  *Robínia pseùdo-acàcia*

*Wistèria sinénsis*
Magnoliàceae (Magnolia Family)
  *Liriodéndron tulipífera*
  *Magnòlia acumìnàta*
  *Magnòlia viginiàna*
Meliàceae (Mahogany Family)
  *Mélia azédarach*
Moràceae (Mulberry Family)
  *Maclùra pomífera*
  *Mòrus rùbra*
Myricàceae (Wax Myrtle Family)
  *Comptònia peregrìna*
  *Myrìca cerífera*
Nyssàceae (Sour Gum Family)
  *Nýssa sylvática*
Oleàceae (Olive Family)
  *Chionánthus virgínicus*
  *Fráxinus americàna*
Pinàceae (Pine Family)
  *Juníperus virginiàna*
  *Pícea rùbens*
  *Pìnus púngens*
  *Pìnus rígida*
  *Pìnus stròbus*
  *Pìnus taèda*
  *Pìnus virginiàna*
  *Taxòdium dístichum*
  *Thùja occidentàlis*
  *Tsùga canadénsis*
Platanàceae (Plane Tree Family)
  *Plátanus occidentàlis*
Rhamnàceae (Buckthorn Family)
  *Ceanòthus americànus*

Rosàceae (Rose Family)
  *Amelánchier arbòrea*
  *Physocárpus opulifòlius*
  *Prùnus seròtina*
  *Pỳrus americàna*
  *Pỳrus arbutifòlia*
  *Rìbes rotundifòlium*
  *Ròsa carolìna*
  *Rùbus odoràtus*
  *Spiraèa japónica*
Rubiàceae (Madder Family)
  *Cephalánthus occidentàlis*
Rutàceae (Rue Family)
  *Ptèlea trifoliàta*
Salicàceae (Willow Family)
  *Pópulus deltoìdes*
  *Sàlix babylónica*
  *Sàlix serícea*
Saxifragàceae (Saxifrage Family)
  *Hydrangèa arboréscens*
Scrophulariàceae (Figwort Family)
  *Paulównia tomentòsa*
Simaroubàceae (Quassia Family)
  *Ailánthus altíssima*
Staphyleàceae (Bladdernut Family)
  *Staphylèa trifòlia*
Tiliàceae (Linden Family)
  *Tília heterophýlla*
Ulmàceae (Elm Family)
  *Céltis laevigàta*
  *Úlmus americàna*

# Index of Common and Scientific Names